PERFORMANCE
EDITIONS

LABORUM
DULCE
LENIMEN

G. SCHIRMER

MOZART
15 EASY PIANO PIECES

Edited by Elena Abend

Also available:
00296685 Mozart: 15 Easy Piano Pieces,
with companion recordings recorded by Elena Abend

Additionally, editor Elena Abend's recordings of the pieces
in this collection are available for purchase on iTunes.

On the cover:
Boy and Girl Dancing Minuet
18th Century, Anonymous

© Bettmann/CORBIS

ISBN 978-1-4950-0728-6

G. SCHIRMER, Inc.

DISTRIBUTED BY

HAL•LEONARD®
CORPORATION
7777 W. BLUEMOUND RD. P.O. BOX 13819 MILWAUKEE, WI 53213

www.musicsalesclassical.com
www.halleonard.com

CONTENTS

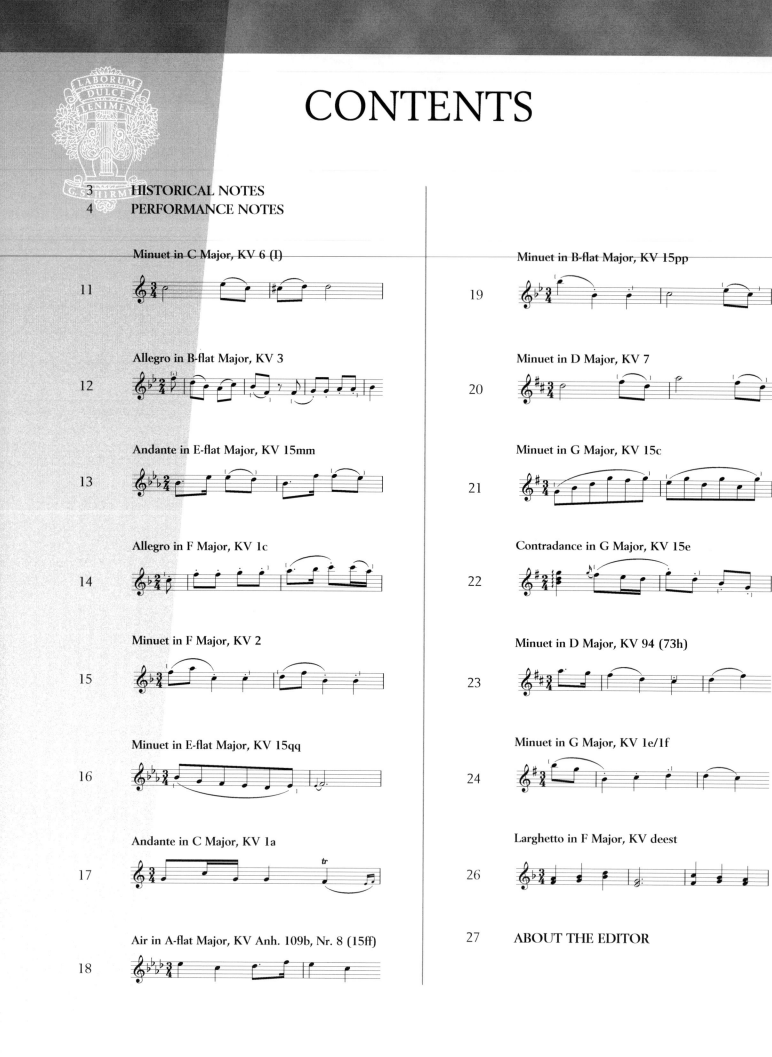

HISTORICAL NOTES

WOLFGANG AMADEUS MOZART (1756-1791)

Many of the pieces in this volume are works that Mozart wrote as a child, and some are among his very earliest compositions. It is fascinating to imagine what early boyhood must have been like for the young Wolfgang Amadeus Mozart. His precocious musical talent was already evident to his father, Leopold, when Wolfgang was as young as four years old. By age six, he was a harpsichord virtuoso and was composing his own music. Leopold, a violinist and composer, was his children's sole teacher, instructing them in all subjects, including music. Wolfgang's earliest original compositions were likely written with his father's assistance, or were heavily edited by his father, though they reveal extraordinary talent.

Leopold was an enterprising man and sought to share the considerable talents of his children with the world. He arranged various concert tours for the family, some lasting as long as three years. They traveled throughout the courts of Europe, with Wolfgang and his older sister, Nannerl, performing on the harpsichord, and Leopold playing the violin. Wolfgang ultimately spent about ten years of his childhood traveling on these concert tours.

The three Mozarts dazzled the courts of Europe, especially young Wolfgang. Aside from playing prepared pieces, he performed a number of tricks, such as playing with the keyboard covered by a cloth and sight-reading difficult music. He also exhibited his astounding memory by playing back pieces that he had heard only once. These skills further expanded in adulthood, when Wolfgang routinely improvised elaborate pieces at the keyboard during concert performances.

Many of the hosts for the family's concerts were kings and queens, including the Empress Maria Theresa and her daughter Maria, who later became Marie-Antoinette of France. Maria Theresa was so delighted with the children's performance that she sent them a set of tiny court clothes as a gift.

During Wolfgang's travels, he was exposed to the most popular musical styles of the day and he met many important composers and performers. Johann Christian Bach was a particular influence on the boy when in London. Mozart heard dance music, chamber ensembles, early examples of symphonies, and operas, which his remarkable brain was then able to assimilate and improve upon in his own works. Even as a child he was a prolific composer, writing concertos, symphonies, sonatas, and operas by the age of 13. Today, his numerous solo piano sonatas and piano concertos remain important staples of the piano repertoire.

—*Susanne Sheston*

PERFORMANCE NOTES

Wolfgang Amadeus Mozart composed the keyboard pieces in this volume during the period from 1761 until 1770; from the time he was a precocious six-year-old to an unusually sophisticated 14-year-old poised for one of the most remarkable careers in music history. Coincidently, many students who perform these works probably fall within the same age range of the boy Mozart. This music is so sophisticated that it is nearly inconceivable that it is the work of a child. Though the pieces are brief, they are all fully conceived compositions, unfailingly elegant in Mozart's innate understanding of voice leading and harmony.

From a pedagogical perspective, the pieces in this publication can serve many purposes. Music of the Classical era, and particularly Mozart's music, lays bare the technique of a pianist much more than a Chopin waltz or a Rachmaninoff prelude. The music has a leanness of texture that exposes any unevenness or technical shortcomings of the performer. Mozart's pieces are perfect compositions that beg to be performed perfectly. Playing them can teach (among other skills) restraint, lightness of touch, and beauty of tone. The challenge is to find the shape and style of each little piece.

Unlike Clementi's *Sonatinas*, Op. 36, which were written specifically as teaching pieces, many of the works in this collection were essentially the young Wolfgang's composition lessons, which were reviewed by his father Leopold. Many of the pieces come from either *Nannerl's Notebook*, a book of compositions Mozart's father Leopold kept for Wolfgang's older sister's piano study, or Mozart's *London Notebook*, a composition notebook Wolfgang kept during the family's performing tour to that city in 1764-65. Very few dynamic or articulation indications are given in urtext sources. (Mozart gave very few such indications in his later works as well, trusting performers to understand the style, typical of the time.) The purpose of this edition is to show

elements of style through editorial additions in the score. Any added markings are placed in brackets. There is a line somewhere between printed recommendations in an edition for the purpose of style and coaching a performance in the score. Listening to a recording particularly with the guidance of a teacher, may allow a student to observe many more details of articulation and phrasing than could be notated.

These pieces can lead a student naturally to some of the easier sonatinas of Clementi and Kuhlau. Also in the Schirmer Performance Editions, this volume will lead progressively into the *15 Intermediate Piano Pieces*, which features music from throughout Mozart's life.

Articulation and Fingering

The piano in Mozart's time was still in its infancy, and had a much looser, more nimble key action. This instrument was conducive to producing a delicate lightness of touch that should be emulated in performances on modern pianos. Additionally, Mozart composed many of his early works for harpsichord and clavichord, both of which have a very limited dynamic range. As a result, clear articulation and phrasing were needed to bring performances to life. Fingering is a vital aspect of finding this sparkle in your playing. Most of the fingering recommendations were made in service to the articulation of a phrase, be it legato, staccato, or portato (see below for explanation of these terms). Articulations in this edition are suggested to bring the style of these pieces to the fore. Fingering has been chosen for the average hand; you may decide to use different fingerings that are more comfortable for a particular player's hands. Regardless of the fingering, it is important to remember that in Classical repertoire, fingering is articulation. The choice of fingering will have a significant impact on the clarity of the articulation and phrasing. For instance, notice the fingering in measure 5 of the "Minuet in B-flat Major" and how it requires the pianist to lift between the printed slurs.

Minuet in B-flat Major, KV 15pp, m. 5

Three basic articulations are found in this volume:

LEGATO

Legato is the Italian word for "bound." Legato playing is usually shown with slurs and requires a smooth connection of the notes with no separation between them.

The notes are "bound" together. In this style of music, in a series of slurred notes, there are slight lifts (or breaths) between the slurs.

STACCATO

Staccato (Italian for "detached") is indicated by a dot over a note. These notes should be shortened considerably from their printed duration. It is important to note that staccato does not mean accented or punched, but simply means short and detached.

PORTATO

Portato is an articulation that lies somewhere between legato and staccato. It requires less separation than true staccato, but is not to be performed smoothly, as in legato playing. It is often notated with slurred staccato markings.

In this edition, there are many instances when a passage might not have any articulation marked at all.

Minuet in C Major, KV 6 (I), mm. 5-8

This and many other similar passages are effectively performed with a portato articulation. It is crucial to understand that portato is the default articulation of Classical style. True staccato and legato are deliberate choices to spell the otherwise constant portato approach. Many pianists encourage blandness in playing music of this period with constant legato playing when portato is the better stylistic choice. It gives the music character and contrast, and produces clarity of texture.

Dynamics

As mentioned above, many pieces in this volume were likely composed for the harpsichord or clavichord, which were limited in their dynamic range. It is important to keep this in mind when performing these works on the modern piano. The clavichord had an especially intimate quality of sound that could never come close to matching the power of today's pianos. Classical restraint is essential to performing the dynamic indications with integrity, even on a modern piano with more dynamic range. The bracketed dynamics are editorial suggestions.

Pedaling

Mozart did not write pedal indications for any of the pieces in this volume. The damper pedal did not start to be used in pianos until very late in the 18th century, after these pieces were written. While pedal should not be arbitrarily banned from performances of this music, it is essential that when the pedal is used, that it is with the utmost discretion. Most, if not all, of the pieces in this volume can be performed satisfactorily without using the damper pedal at all. Removing the crutch of the pedal will force your fingers to find clear, elegant intentions, which the pedal often blurs when not used with taste. One might use a little pedal in the "Larghetto in F Major," (see example) to help with legato phrasing, but it should never impede the clarity of the harmony or the melodic line. Experiment with depressing the pedal only one-half or one-quarter of the full depth to avoid choppiness and unwanted extra noise from the dampers.

Larghetto in F Major, KV deest, mm. 1-4

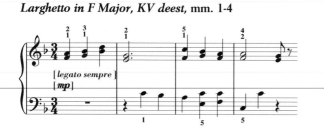

Ornamentation

Appoggiaturas, acciaccaturas, and trills abound in this music and add to its grace and style. Appoggiaturas are indicated by grace notes without a slash through them, and are generally performed in a lyrical manner, on the beat in the Classical era, not before it. Acciaccaturas (possibly from the Italian *acciaccare*, to crush) are indicated by grace notes with a slash, and normally only appear in pieces with a quick tempo. They should be played quickly, "crushed" in just before the beat, almost simultaneous with the principal note. In this edition the execution of all ornaments is notated above the music staff at the relevant points. Trills generally start from the note above in music of this period, often with a concluding *Nachschlag* (termination).

 It is important that ornaments not be thought of arbitrarily as "fast notes." They need to fit the style and tempo of the music. A trill in the "Air in A-flat Major" is performed in a more subdued manner than the sparkling trill in the "Minuet in G Major."

Air in A-flat Major, KV 15ff, m. 7

Minuet in G Major, KV 1e/1f, m. 7

Tempo

In many pieces in this collection, there were no tempo indications written by Mozart. We have placed tempo suggestions in brackets for those pieces that did not have such indications. Additionally, a suggested metronome marking is indicated at the beginning of each piece. These markings are suggestions only. Tempo is a particularly subjective aspect of interpretation, with no two pianists likely to choose the exact same tempo for a piece. But how does one chose an appropriate tempo? This is a challenging question that faces students and teachers. With pieces that are dances (minuets, contradances, etc.), knowing something about how that dance is performed will assist in choosing the proper tempo and style. From a purely technical point of view, you can isolate the most difficult section of a piece, or the section with the most moving notes, to determine which tempo will work best for that passage, then apply that to the entire piece. Be sensitive to an appropriate aesthetic of Classical restraint in choosing a tempo. Find a tempo that will bring the organic elegance of these pieces to life. Extremes of tempo should be avoided and steadiness is crucial. Unlike Chopin's music, with its fluidity and rubato, varying the tempo in a Mozart piece, except at rare and deliberate points, destroys the essence of the music. Mozart wrote the following in a letter to his father from Augsburg on October 24, 1777: "Nannette Stein [a young musical prodigy from Augsburg] will never acquire the most essential, the most difficult and the chief requisite in music, which is, time, because from her earliest years she has done her utmost not to play in time…Everyone is amazed that I can always keep strict time."[1] Only very occasionally do we suggest a *poco rit.* or a fermata in this edition.

Style

Style is the most important element in a performance of Mozart's music, and in many ways is the most difficult to define. These little pieces hold importance and interest for students and concert artists. They are complete, satisfying little miniatures that show the innocence of Mozart's youth, but are still incredibly sophisticated. Their style is the fusion of dynamics, articulation, and tempo together with Classical restraint and technique. Mozart's style has a lively elegance that comes from the crystalline texture of his music, along with his supreme gift as a melodist. Mozart is quoted in *The Reminiscences of Michael Kelly*, 1826, saying that "Melody is the essence of music."[2] He valued this quality above all others in music. His phrases beg to be sung. Mozart was, after all, one of the greatest vocal composers. Phrasing is key in performing his music, understanding how each phrase builds and eventually tapers to its conclusion, and interacts and leads into the next phrase. In the first four measures of the Andante in E-flat Major we see an example of how this works. The first phrase (from measures one through four) builds to a peak and tapers to the end. Hairpin dynamics are suggested to assist in making this phrase effective.

Andante in E-flat Major, KV 15mm, mm. 1-4

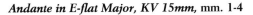

Don't confuse slurs with phrasing. Slurs are about articulation, not broader shape. Imagine listening to an actor in a play who never observed the commas or periods written in the script. Their performance would be, at best, bland and at worst, completely unintelligible. You can think of slurs as clauses within a larger musical sentence, the phrase. As you can see in the example above there are many small slurs contained within one overarching phrase. This concept of building to a peak and releasing can be applied to many pieces and phrases in this book. This should not be an exaggerated effect. Exaggeration is not a part of this style. Even when there are *subito* changes in dynamic, they are performed in a more restrained manner than would be expected in Romantic music.

Minuets

Mozart composed many minuets in his early years, several of which are included in this edition. The minuet (sometimes also spelled menuet) is a restrained, complex, and elegant dance, which has its origins in France It has a stately, aristocratic quality and was most popular from 1650 until 1800. Dance often inspired art music, particularly in the Baroque era when entire suites of dances such as bourrées, minuets, musettes, polonaises, and sarabandes were composed by J. S. Bach and others. The minuet was the only Baroque dance to survive past 1750. Not surprisingly, after the French Revolution and the death of the aristocracy, the minuet faded into history, not to return until the Neo-Classical movement of the early 20th century. The minuet is considerably different from the waltz, another famous dance in 3/4 time. The minuet generally has a slower, more deliberate tempo than a waltz, with a shortness of articulation on beats two or three leading to a strong downbeat. The articulations suggested in this edition attempt to create this minuet style.

A Note on Teaching Order and Köchel Numbers

The pieces in this edition are presented in a suggested teaching order, with the works becoming more difficult through the book. The pieces are identified by their Köchel or KV numbers Mozart's compositions were first catalogued by Ludwig Köchel, who published the first edition of his findings in 1862 (KV stands for Köchel-Verzeichnes, after the title of the original publication). The catalogue has undergone significant revisions since then, with the most recent edition appearing in 1964. In some cases, the composition dates of certain pieces have been changed due to continued Mozart research. As a result, a few pieces in this edition have two KV numbers. The first KV number is the original number from the first edition of the catalogue, and the second KV number is from the sixth edition (1964).

Notes on the Individual Pieces

NANNERL'S NOTEBOOK

Mozart's older sister, Nannerl, began keyboard studies at age seven, when Wolfgang was three years old. She became an accomplished musician in her own right, and was a full participant in the musical tours the family took during the 1760s. Leopold Mozart gave her this notebook for practicing. It contained several pieces arranged in progressive order by contemporary composers, including Leopold Mozart himself. As a toddler Wolfgang was entranced by instruments and entertained himself by picking out intervals at the keyboard. By the time Mozart was four years old, he was learning to play some of the pieces in the notebook. Leopold Mozart notated in the pages when and how long it would take Wolfgang to master a particular piece. By the end of 1761, when Mozart was six years old, Leopold wrote down Wolfgang's first compositions as he played them. There is nothing crude about these early pieces; each is its own little jewel. There is a freshness of sound about them compared to other adult composers of the era.

Allegro in B-flat Major, KV 3

This little piece is dated March 1762 and was written in Salzburg. The form is ABA'. The first A section cadences in F major, the dominant of B-flat major. The melodic material of the A section is developed in the B section before the A section returns in a modified version at the upbeat to measure 21. The piece is almost entirely written in only two voices, with a third voice added only to reinforce the tonic chord in measures 4, 6, 24, and 26. We have suggested many articulations in this piece. Without some guidance in this regard, it will not have a lively sense of style. Be particularly vigilant in performing the two-note slurs gracefully, avoiding the temptation to play with a legato touch.

Allegro in F Major, KV 1c

A march-like quality pervades this piece, dated by Leopold Mozart as being written on December 11, 1761 in Salzburg. It is in ABA form and is written in two voices throughout. Notice the echoing dynamics that we suggest to bring interest to the repetitions of the melodic material. You can work on independence of the hands as well, carefully observing the right hand slurs against the staccato accompaniment in the left hand. One can perhaps imagine the five-year-old Mozart playing soldier in this piece!

Minuet in F Major, KV 2

This piece was written during January 1762 in Salzburg. The form is ABA', with repeats. The opening A section returns at measure 18 in a slightly modified version. This is a tightly knit composition, with the opening rhythmic motive which is stated in the first measure appearing in all but six measures. Observe carefully the suggested articulations, particularly the staccato notes on beats two and three. This will give the minuet an irresistible, dance-like quality.

Andante in C Major, KV 1a

This brief piece is Mozart's first recorded composition, written in late January or early February 1761 in Salzburg, around his fifth birthday. It is in an unusual AB form, with the A section written in 3/4 time and the B section written in 2/4 time. It is a courtly little composition, with lightly accompanied, periodic melodies. There are echoes of the Baroque in the final six measures. Gracefulness is essential in performing the piece; the ornaments should not be heavy-handed. We suggest echoing dynamics for the first four measures, to bring interest to the repeated melodic material.

Minuet in D Major, KV 7

This minuet comes from a Sonata in C Major that Wolfgang composed for keyboard with optional violin accompaniment (a popular genre at the time). The violin parts in compositions such as these were purely accompaniment, and the sonatas are satisfactorily performed by keyboard only. This movement appears in Nannerl's Notebook in a keyboard only version with a composition date of November 23, 1763 in Paris. As in all the minuets in this edition, careful attention to the suggested articulation and dynamics will give the music the lightness and clarity that it needs.

Minuet in G Major, KV 1e/1f

This piece actually combines two pieces from Nannerl's Notebook into a minuet and trio form. The trio originated in the Baroque period as a contrast to the minuet. It was often performed by three players (hence trio). These pieces were likely composed in late 1761 or early 1762 in Salzburg. Both the minuet and trio are written in ABA' form with repeats. The minuet style is shown through the suggested articulations in the music.

THE LONDON NOTEBOOK

The London Notebook, from which many of the pieces in this edition are drawn, was a musical sketchbook that Mozart kept during his time in London from April 1764 through August 1765. It is identified in the most recent Köchel catalogue as KV 15. Leopold Mozart was very ill during July and August of 1764, during which time all public performances were cancelled. It is possible that Wolfgang used this time to work in this notebook. It contains 43 pieces of varying levels of completeness. We see the young composer experimenting with phrase structure and extending his musical themes compared to his earlier compositions from *Nannerl's Notebook*. The pieces are sparsely ornamented in general, keeping in the *style galant** aesthetic of the times. Mozart explores the minor tonality extensively for the first time in this notebook. Though they may have been composition exercises, they feel like complete pieces. The music almost always has a playfulness about it. The notebook was dated 1764 on its cover, and modern scholarship believes that the pieces contained within were written either in 1764 or 1765.

*The style galant movement appeared in the early to mid-18th century as a reaction against the strict, contrapuntal music of the Baroque era and was exemplified by composers such as Johann Christian Bach. Galant music is characterized by a lightness of texture, short phrases, and simple harmony with frequent cadences.

Andante in E-flat Major, KV 15mm

This song-like Andante is written in ABA form. We recommend a *piano* dynamic throughout this piece due to the serene stillness that the music suggests. Use this piece to work on a smooth legato touch, and gracefully taper the ends of each phrase.

Minuet in E-flat Major, KV 15qq

This piece is written in ABA' form. The first four measures of the A section are not repeated when the A section returns in measure 13. Rather, the second four measures of the A section are played a perfect fourth higher, closing the piece in the tonic key of E-flat major. The rolled chords that appear in measures 5 and 6, as well as 13 and 14, are an unusual characteristic of this piece. They should be played with the utmost clarity.

Air in A-flat Major, K. 15ff

This is a melodically driven piece in simple AB form, with repeats. It has a serene perfection throughout, with no tension present. It demands an even touch and a lyrical sweetness to the playing. Be conscious of creating a true legato sound and taper phrases elegantly. Play the trills at a slower speed, consistent with the still mood of the piece.

Minuet in B-flat Major, KV 15pp

This form of this piece is ABA'. The dramatic opening motive of the falling octave is immediately followed by a gracefully lyric phrase. Articulation is crucial in bringing this dance movement to life. Make clear contrasts between the staccato and slurred passages.

Minuet in G Major, KV 15c

This minuet is in ABA' form. When the A section returns at measure 13, it eventually cadences in the tonic, and not the dominant, as it does in measure 8. This piece will reward those students who practice their scales and arpeggios diligently. Teachers have their reasons for assigning those exercises! The opening melodic figure, and other similar arpeggio-based passages require perfect evenness. We suggest that the left hand assist the right hand in the large intervallic leaps in measures 5 and 6 (indicated in the score) as well as in measure 17, by playing both notes on the downbeat, allowing the right hand time to gracefully play the remaining eighth notes in those measures.

Contradance in G Major, KV 15e

A contradance is a fast dance in 2/4 or 2/2 time, built upon repeated eight-measure phrases. Inspired by English peasant country dances, this form became popular with the European aristocracy during the late 17th and 18th centuries. Mozart wrote many such dances, as did Beethoven, in a set of 12 he published in 1802. This contradance is built on eight-measure sections, and has a form of ABA', with repeats. Only the second half of the A section is repeated at the end of the piece, this time in G major instead of D major. There must be a strong contrast between the slurred passages and the light, staccato passages to perform this dance effectively.

OTHER PIECES

Minuet in C Major, KV 6 (I)

This minuet comes from a Sonata in C Major that Wolfgang composed for keyboard with optional violin accompaniment. It was first published in February 1764 in Paris as Op. 1, No. 1, and was dedicated to Madame Victoire de France, the second daughter of Louis XV. The Mozart family was staying in Paris at the time, seeking performances at court and for other nobility. The piece is in AB form with repeats, with the last four measures of the B section replicating the last four measures of the A section, written a perfect fifth lower. The minuet style is less defined in this music than in other Mozart minuets. It is written in two voices only. Imagine the individual voices being played by a violin and cello. How would the phrasing sound? Try to emulate the singing tone of stringed instruments in your playing, particularly in the right hand melody.

Minuet in D Major, KV 94 (73h)

This piece was composed in either March or April 1770 when Mozart was on a trip to Italy. It was likely composed in Bologna or Rome. Leopold and Wolfgang traveled to Italy in 1770 not only for Mozart to perform, but also as part of his education, to travel to the roots of opera. The form of this minuet is ABA', with repeats. The piece starts out in strict canon, with the left hand imitating the right. The right and left hands must operate completely independently with regards to phrasing and articulation. Play the 16th notes with a distinct, but slight accent.

Larghetto in F Major, KV deest

This piece is not listed in the latest edition of the Köchel catalogue (any piece labeled "KV deest" does not have a KV number assigned to it at this time). It does appear in the Appendix of the 1964 edition in Ahnang B, page 805. It may have been written in the mid-1770s based on the maturity

of the harmony and musical ideas. The form is ABA', with repeats. The texture is similar to a string quartet, with four clearly defined voices. It should be legato throughout, with a quiet, lyric quality. The opening right hand melody, built on thirds, moves to the left hand at the beginning of the B section in measure 9, with the right hand offering its ornamented commentary. When the A section returns at measure 17, it is a variation of the opening section, with a poignant deceptive cadence at measure 24. The work concludes with a brief coda, ending with the same sighing phrase found in measures 7 and 8.

—Elena Abend, editor
and Christopher Ruck, assistant editor

Notes

1. Marshall, Robert L. *Mozart Speaks: Views on Music, Musicians, and the World.* (New York: Schirmer Books, 1991), 202

2. *Ibid.,* 196.

Suggested Reading

Marshall, Robert L. *Mozart Speaks: Views on Music, Musicians, and the World.* New York: Schirmer Books, 1991.

Rosen, Charles. The Classical Style: Haydn, Mozart, Beethoven. exp. ed. New York: W. W. Norton, 1997.

Sadie, Stanley. *Mozart: The Early Years 1756-1781.* New York: W. W. Norton & Company, 2006.

Soloman, Maynard. *Mozart: A Life.* New York: HarperCollins, 1995.

Spaethling, Robert. *Mozart's Letters, Mozart's Life.* New York: W. W. Norton & Company, 2000.

Minuet

Wolfgang Amadeus Mozart
KV 6 (I)

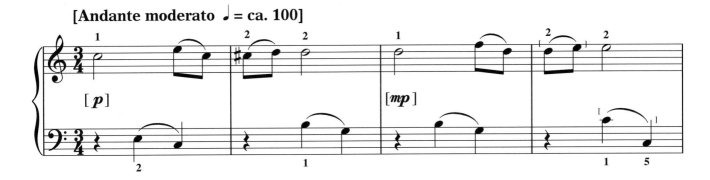

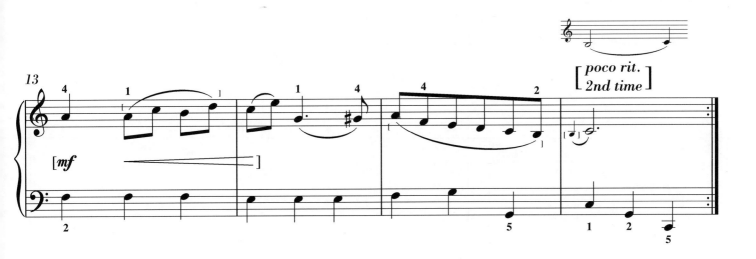

Allegro

Wolfgang Amadeus Mozart
KV 3

Allegro [♩ = ca. 120-126]

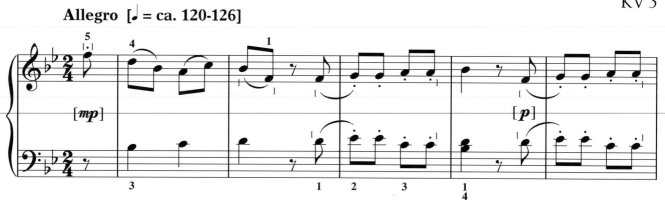

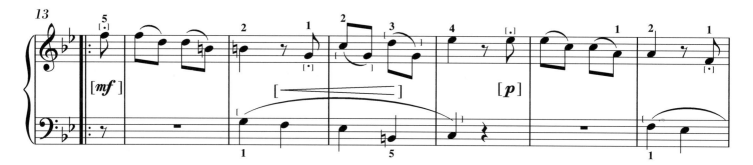

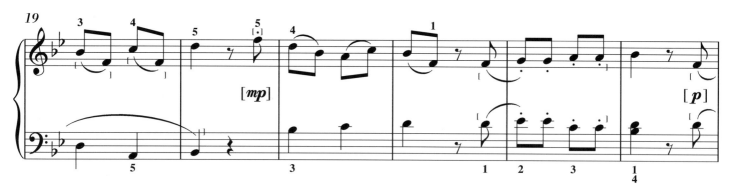

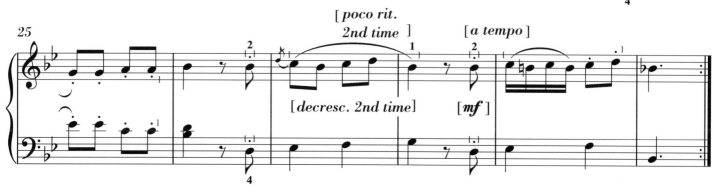

Andante

Wolfgang Amadeus Mozart
KV 15mm

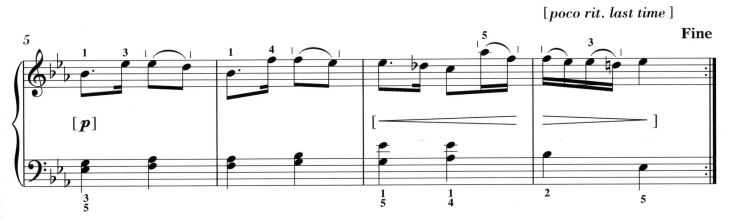

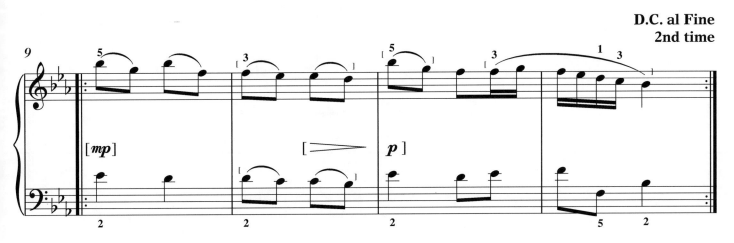

Eliminate the repeat on the Da Capo.

Allegro

Wolfgang Amadeus Mozart
KV 1c

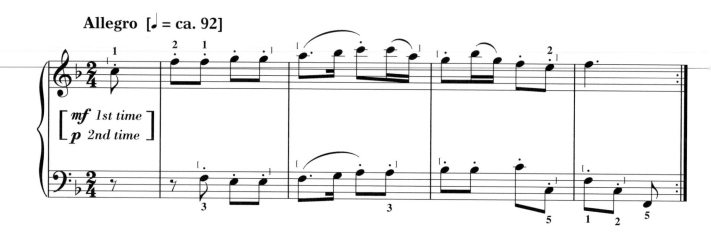

Minuet

Wolfgang Amadeus Mozart
KV 2

[Allegretto ♩ = ca. 108]

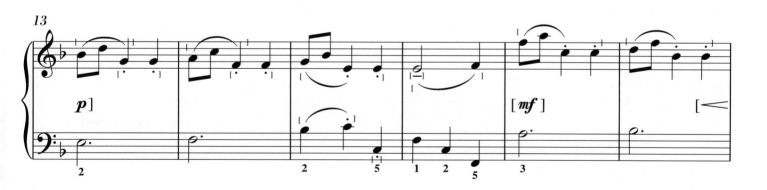

[poco rit.]   [a tempo]

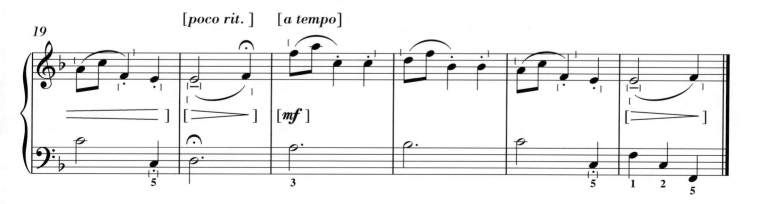

Minuet

Wolfgang Amadeus Mozart
KV 15qq

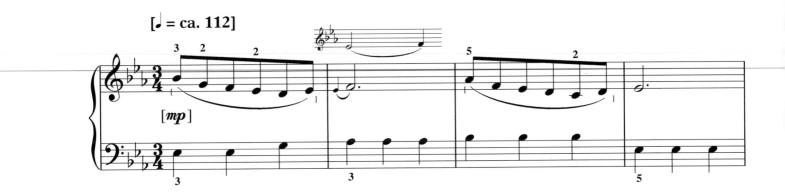

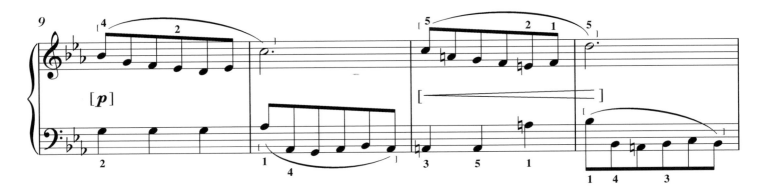

*Played:

Andante

Wolfgang Amadeus Mozart
KV 1a

Andante [♩ = ca. 56]

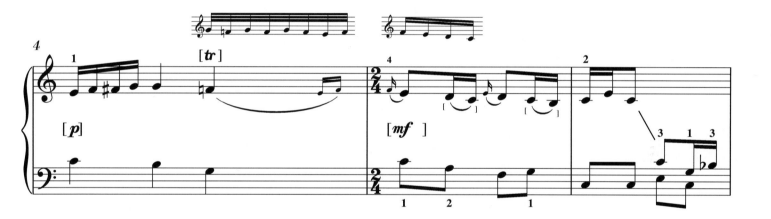

Air

Wolfgang Amadeus Mozart
KV Anh. 109b Nr. 8 (15ff)

[Andante ♩ = ca. 88]

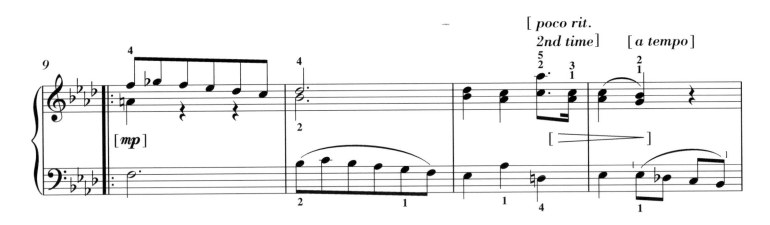

Minuet

Wolfgang Amadeus Mozart
KV 15pp

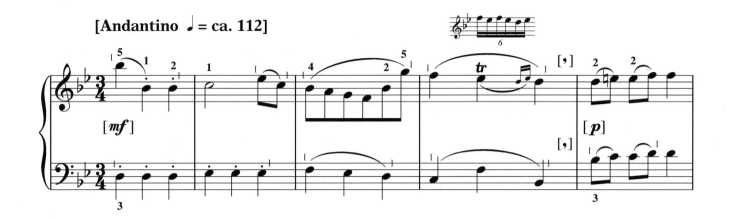

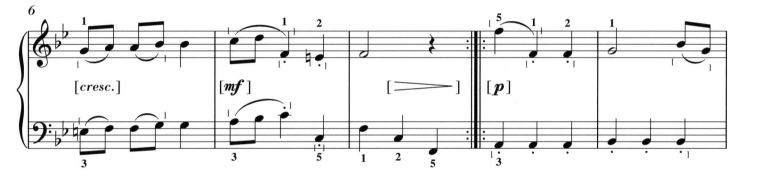

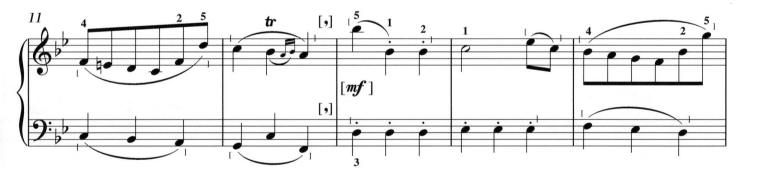

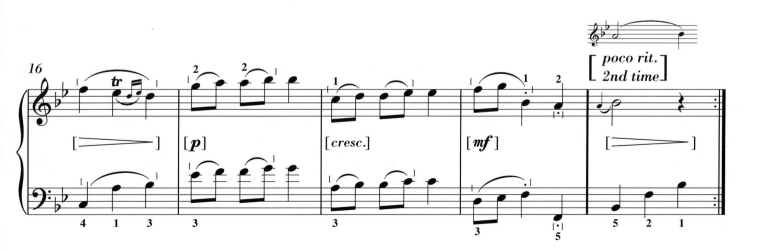

Minuet

Wolfgang Amadeus Mozart
KV 7

[Andante con moto ♩ = ca. 116-120]

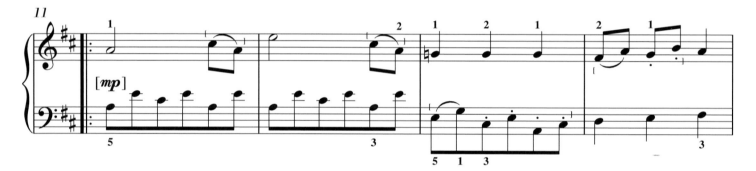

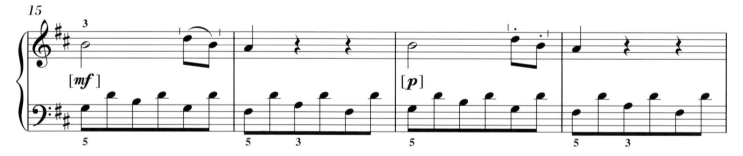

* optional trill

Minuet

Wolfgang Amadeus Mozart
KV 15c

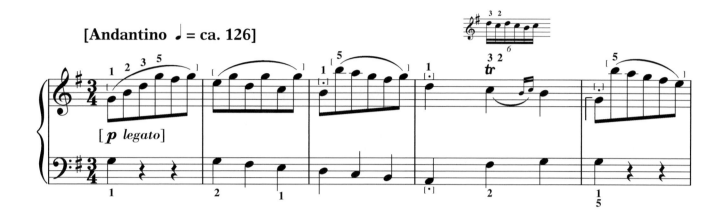

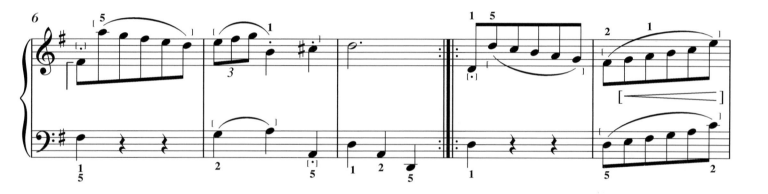

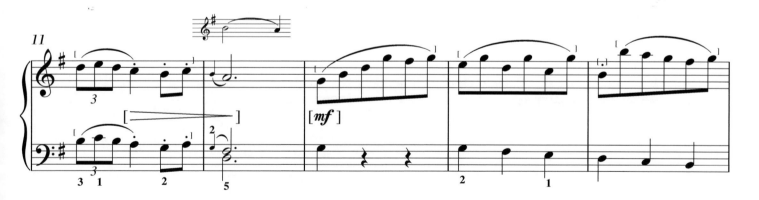

Contradance

Wolfgang Amadeus Mozart
KV 15e

[Allegro ♩ = ca. 108]

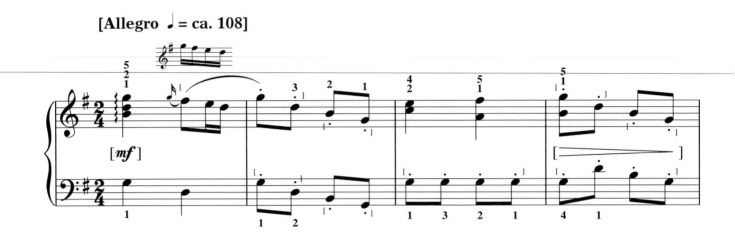

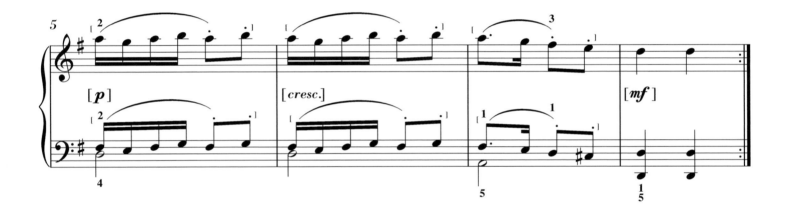

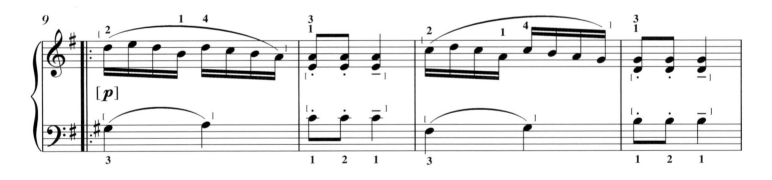

Minuet

Wolfgang Amadeus Mozart
KV 94 (73h)

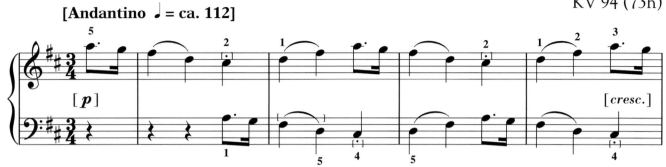

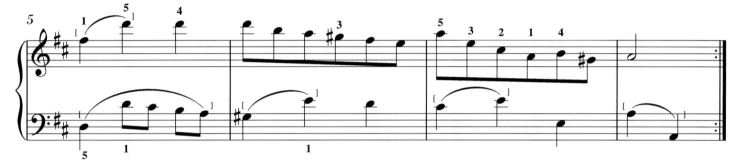

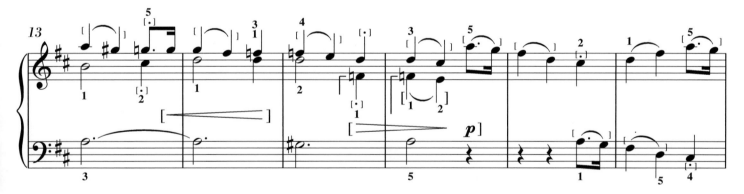

* Mozart originally wrote:

We have raised the lower voice one octave to facilitate this passage for student pianists.

Minuet

Wolfgang Amadeus Mozart
KV le/lf

[Andante ♩ = ca. 126]

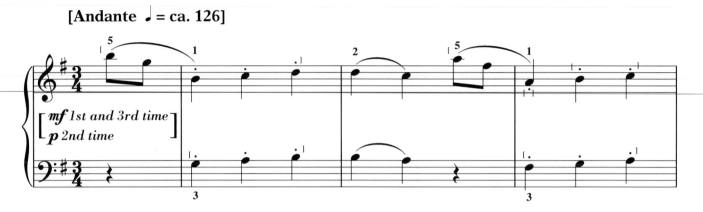

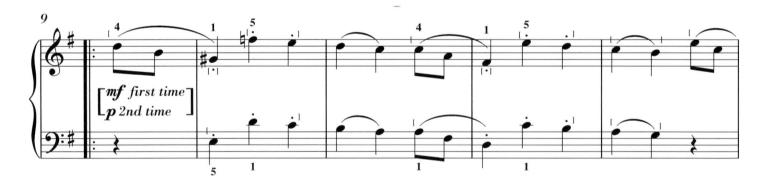

Fine
[*poco rit. last time*]

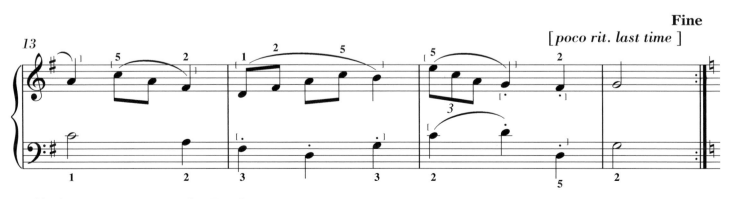

Eliminate repeats on the Da Capo.

Trio

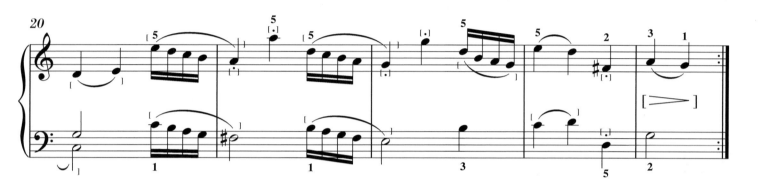

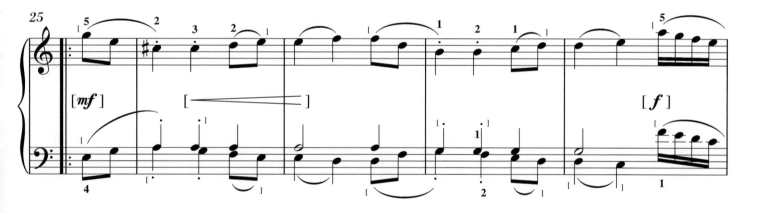

D.C. al Fine
second time

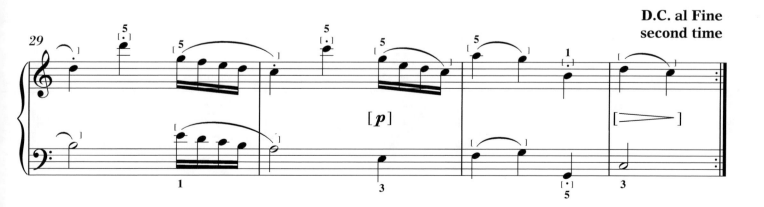

Larghetto

Wolfgang Amadeus Mozart
KV deest

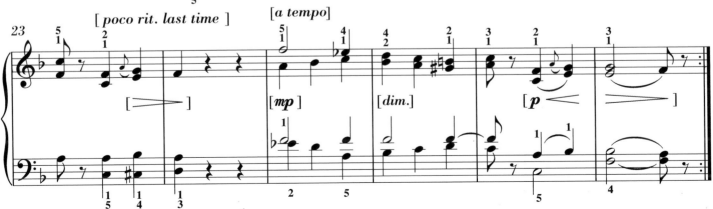

ABOUT THE EDITOR

Elena Abend

Born in Caracas, Venezuela, pianist Elena Abend is well known as a soloist and chamber musician. She has performed with all the major orchestras of her country and has recorded with the Filarmonica Nacional. As the recipient of a scholarship from the Venezuelan Council for the Arts, Abend studied at the Juilliard School, where she received her Bachelor and Master degrees. She has performed at the Purcell Room in London's Royal Festival Hall, Avery Fisher Hall in New York's Lincoln Center, Weill Recital Hall at Carnegie Hall and the Academy of Music with the Philadelphia Orchestra. Other engagements have included the Wigmore Hall in London, the Toulouse Conservatoire in France, the Corcoran Gallery in Washington DC, the United Nations, Merkin Concert Hall in New York, Chicago Cultural Center, the Pabst Theater in Milwaukee, the Atlanta Historical Society, the Teresa Carreno Cultural Center in Caracas, as well as the Theatre Luxembourg in Meaux, France. Other chamber music collaborations include numerous performances at the Ravinia and Marlboro Music Festivals, as well as live broadcasts on Philadelphia's WFLN, The Dame Myra Hess Concert Series on Chicago's WFMT and Wisconsin Public Radio at the Elvehjem Museum in Madison, Wisconsin. Abend has been on the Faculty of the Wisconsin Conservatory of Music, Indiana University's String Academy summer program and the Milwaukee Chamber Music Festival. She has also performed on the Milwaukee Chamber Orchestra Series at Schwan Concert Hall, Piano Chamber, New Generations, Music from Almost Yesterday and the Yolanda Marculescu Vocal Art Series at the University of Wisconsin. She has performed with the "Rembrandt Chamber Players" of Chicago, "Present Music Now," "Frankly Music," and the Fine Arts Quartet on several occasions. A newly released CD with clarinetist Todd Levy, performing the two Brahms Sonatas and the Schumann Fantasy and Romance pieces, is now available on the Avie label. She has also recorded extensively in the *Schirmer Instrumental Library* series for G. Schirmer. She is on the music faculty at the University of Wisconsin-Milwaukee.